Standing Before Yo*u*

Maholi Diaz

Copyright © 2025 Maholi Diaz
All rights reserved

ISBN: 9798317461027
Safe Creatives Registration: 2506182167718

Illustrations and cover designed by @maholi.diaz
No use of this work is permitted without the express permission of the author

If sharing a brief quotation or poem on social media,
please credit the author Maholi Diaz and tag the author's Instagram
@maholi.diaz when possible

Do not alter or resell content
Thank you for helping this book reach others in its full truth and spirit

: Standing Before You

to…

those who love me
those who hate me
and the one that will save me

Standing Before You

content

actions	9
emotions	21
people	47
neglect	67
letters	83
spanish	105
final note	135
book one	136
thank you	137
daily journal	138
recommendations	139
about the author	140

"We don't read and write poetry because it's cute.
We read and write poetry because we are members of the human race.
And the human race is filled with passion.
And medicine, law, business, engineering, these are noble pursuits and necessary to sustain life.
But poetry, beauty, romance, love, these are what we stay alive for. To quote from Whitman, "O me! O life!... of the questions of these recurring; of the endless trains of the faithless... of cities filled with the foolish; what good amid these, o me, o life?". Answer. That you are here - that life exists, and identity; that the powerful play goes on and you may contribute a verse. That the powerful play *goes on* and you may contribute a verse.

What will your verse be?"

- John Keating. Dead Poets Society. -

this time… with intention.
this is my verse

Standing Before You

actions

...

Standing Before You

chapter reflection

self-love is not easy or flashy
it's brushing your hair
when no one sees you
and making coffee
when you feel like disappearing
being grateful for breathing in and out
that's where love starts

Standing Before You

life is to move

if movement is needed
for us to create action
why are we so afraid
to move forward, creating traction?
action demands we let go of self-doubt
away from the silence and boldly step out

is it the unknown
that binds us in place? or
the shadows of failure
we are fearful to face

in the stillness
we admire the road ahead
dreams are yet to be lived
so many words left unsaid

perhaps, it's the comfort
of what we now know
the familiar, the routine
in which we grow slow
so, why do we tremble
at the thought of the new?
forgetting that courage
can carry us through

in the end it's movement that shapes our fate
fear is just something we must mitigate
let us then rise with love in our hearts
hold the unknown as each journey starts

for action is life, and life is to move
make one step today. i believe in you

Standing Before You

chase moments

happiness is a second
a fleeting glimpse of light
the perfect piece of marble
lost in the sculptor's sight

in the end, it disappears
blends with what it was:
a dandelion in the breeze
a memory that passed

happiness fades when grasped
like passing age, like shifting sand

a pursuit, not a destination
a journey, not a location
nothing truly changes

save the endless chase
embrace the joy or sorrow
in every breath you borrow

this fleeting moment
i'll cherish it with you

a second of pure happiness
a glimpse of something true

Standing Before You

you have you

in the absence of external support
the love you have for yourself
must come in the purest form

unprotected youth

if you are lucky
and work hard enough
you will become the guardian
you once longed for…

…and that's beautiful

Standing Before You

music and exercise

music and exercise
are my constant saviours
in this brief journey
where minds collide

they've saved me millions
lifted my soul
kept my heart beating
kept me, sort of, whole

when shadows linger
and hope seems thin
a song or a sprint pulls me back in

the rhythm makes my heartbeat
setting me free... waking me up
showing the strength
deep in my bones

in melodies i sleep
and in movements, i wake

through highs and lows
i find the peace i need to grow
they light the way
saving me still, day by day

challenge

challenge who you are
challenge your opinions

become a unique force
be one in a million

absorb the viewpoints
coming from all directions

identify your flaws
we are exempt from perfection

Standing Before You

don't give up

working on yourself
what does it even mean?

it's finding the broken pieces
you have inside, unseen

reading, learning
breaking yourself a bit more
so all the broken pieces
go back to being whole

in the end
you will know what you want
who you are
and have a plan

being broken
is just the start of a new path

Standing Before You

repeat this when you forget who you are…

I AM BRAVE

DON'T BE AFRAID

DON'T LOSE YOUR PATH

HAVE FAITH

Standing Before You

opportunity

i opened one window
locked the big door
keeping only the real inside
outside nothing more

a smaller circle
love with intention
my body reserved
for forever connection

forgetting the past
embracing what's new
this year
i'm choosing what's true

Standing Before You

what are you hiding?

say it
say it out loud
i need to hear it
you need to hear it

let it come out

don't try to hide it anymore
what we both know

let it breathe
let it come out

say it out loud

Standing Before You

emotions

...

Standing Before You

Standing Before You

chapter reflection

no one says how painful
it can be to feel, in a healthy way
to not hide parts of yourself
life is hard so we will suffer

but we can learn to
hold space for our emotions
learn to tame the impulses
without dimming your essence

i'm learning to
understand myself in fuller ways
to let feelings flow rather than erupt
to feel slowly and steadily
instead of bottling up until i break again

others or myself

Standing Before You

Standing Before You

ducks in a pond

when you are drowning
and everyone else is drowning as well
how do we save each other?
if we are all ducks
paddling hard in a big pond
can we trust, each other's currents
will cause us to bond?
that drops on our feathers
won't carry the ache?

can we be side by side
learning the rainfall
sounds just like a song?
that makes us breathe
feeling less alone

can we stay afloat,
and quietly believe
that being close
won't make us grieve?

not in all spaces
will we be seen
sometimes the search
will replace peace with grief
asking for help
might feel like drowning again

maybe our own feathers
drenched and worn,
aren't holding weight
but something warm

Standing Before You

if i could remember more clearly

how my laughter sounded in childhood play
how my steps felt so clumsy, dearly
how my eyes lit up at the stars on display

if i could look at the past without mist
see my mother with dreams still unspoken
sit beside her, become her closest friend
tell her, "you're not alone, i'm here"

if i could dance with my grandmother
ask her in secret about the love she wanted
whether she ever doubted, whether she cried
whether she dreamed of someone who never arrived

if i could hug my father as a boy
and see in his laughter my own kind of joy
play in his shadow, run through the field
watch the strong man as a child, soft and real

how different this map of the soul would be
if our memories lived with more clarity
if the golden days didn't fade so fast
beneath the quiet weight of years gone past

but maybe, in what we can't recall
lives a mystery the heart feels after all
and in every gesture, in the way i love
an echo of them lingers, quietly enough

so even if i can't see it all
i carry their stories, sky-written and true
and with every step i take, unaware
they walk beside me... always there

Standing Before You

for the you who cries at night

for the you
who still cries at night
when you think no one cares
and feel the world forgets your name

when you stare at the ceiling
hoping someone, somewhere
is thinking of you

when the weight of everything
comes at once
and you wonder
if you'll ever feel light again

i wrote this
so you'd know
you are not forgotten
not invisible
not alone

you can rise again, once more

Standing Before You

not enough

walking, thinking,
the wind in my hair

hoping i am enough
to sweep you away

to carry us both
to the stardust above

where longing meets light
and dreams become love

Standing Before You

share it

i know it doesn't make sense
but trust me
softness is your strength
so share it

the right ones
will lean in, not leave
they'll see you
and breathe themselves
in relief

they'll love you more
for all you give
the truth in your heart
the way that you give in

the secret of life

i think the mistake we make
is thinking we must choose
between chaos and peace
between oldness and youth

i feel the secret of life
it's making peace with both
in duality lies life
and we are full of both

a balance in sight
it's what we must embrace:
the peaceful touch of feathers
on a fire-burning place

for often our life holds storm
but also the sun creeps out in mourn
and it's in the balance of loving each part
that we find what life's about

Standing Before You

the goodbye kiss

everyone remembers their first kiss
do you remember your last?
do you remember the last kiss
you gave with hope?
what was meant to be forever
now no longer loves

His whisper

some poems are meant to reach you
and never be seen again
not even by your own mind

it's like God is playing a game
giving you a gift for you to see
the magic inside your heart
but not to share it with anyone
just for your delight

Standing Before You

a spark that stayed (three-part poem)

in an empty room, our eyes entwined
a spark too vivid to confine

few words were exchanged
and no need for names
yet, in that moment, the world was flames

the noise of life felt still
your quiet pull, a silent plea
lost in the pulse of what could be

you slipped away; a shadow passed
yet the change you left is vast
no numbers sought, no vows made
still, something stayed

a stranger's face, a hidden door
i crave what i've never known
though you are gone, the spark ignited
a mystery burned into my dream nights

Standing Before You

a spark that stayed – part II

dreaming with your smile
a spark so true
your gentle voice
that pulled me through

your subtle presence
soft as a breeze
a missing youth
that never flees

i hold on tight
to the thoughts of you
you were the dream
that i couldn't pursue

i lose myself
when i miss you
regret's a shadow
but facts remain
in every wish
you ease the pain

Standing Before You

a spark that stayed – part III

i saw you once, me passing by
no makeup there to hide or try
your smile was soft
your eyes were kind
as if you saw what's on my mind

you noticed me, or so it seemed
in a moment where my heart dreamed

few words were spoken
the silence was broken

now, all i have is just the thought of you
and all the hopes i've caught with you
no name, no way to tag the space
just memories of your warm embrace

i wonder if you think of me
or if that moment slipped
a chance that vanished
like a soft touch with you

still, i hold on to those
for though you're gone
the thought remains

perhaps one day, the stars align
until then, you're a dream of mine

Standing Before You

joy

i'm trying to remember
the last time joy was pure and clear
it seems as we grow older
joy slips faster year by year

as children, smiles come every day
but grown, joy's moments quickly fly away
we chase new trials along the river
while happy seconds, whisper

so what's the secret, can you tell?
is it gratitude the key to, see?
aware of breath, just simply be?
perhaps the answer's soft and true…

…to find the light inside of you

Standing Before You

what i want

my dream is to find love that's whole
that turns my head but feeds the soul
a person who sees what lies in store
beyond appearance, looking for more

a love so strong
it heals the ache
rebuilds the flame
that doesn't break

a love untouched by time or sin
forever strong, though years grow thin

in the meantime, i will confess
i'll hold my breath for nothing less

Standing Before You

the fortress of logic

my self-defense, a wall so high
where nothing stirs, no need to cry
i numb my feelings, keep them trapped
in this hollow place, beyond good nights

no waves of sorrow, can touch me here
no hurt can reach, what i refuse to see
logic and reason, my sturdy shield
push the pain away, let nothing near

i feel clever in this guarded space
where no emotion dares to leave trace
but still, behind the clever mask
a silent heart yearns but does not dare to ask

Standing Before You

i pressed my lips too hard
with the thought of you…

Standing Before You

thirst

who knew thirst could lead to more
awaken love, i can't ignore
a giant sleeping in my heart
now stirred and longing impact

though outside strong
i stand so tall
inside, i'm soft
i feel it all

so willing now, with love to give
in mellow waves, i start to live
the walls, once high, now start to fall
i give in full. i give my all

thirst brought more, i now confess
awakened love, in tenderness

Standing Before You

tinder

timber fades away
if you don't build a structure
for fire to last

dizzy in lust
we burned before we began

Standing Before You

we are stones

nostalgia shapes a heart in vain
we love the hurt, deny the pain

addicted deep
a constant drip
we cling to cracks
that always slip

it runs through faults
we never admit
our won chosen, gravity

Standing Before You

big hearts

i still don't know how we do it
stay far from our families for so long
yet carry on with a smile

are we just moving on autopilot?
or is it simply who we are?
fighters by nature
made to endure and fight

i feel a love so deep, for life
for the wellbeing of all
for my dreams to fly

for the chance to keep going

still...
there's a little hole in my heart
that seems to grow
each time i miss them all

but thanks to them
my heart knows how to grow bigger

Standing Before You

tonight

i just want for the tears to drop
no half hearts given, but a lonely life forgiven

let the silence speak where voices fail
let the ache be seen without the need to explain
not fixed, not filled... just held

for once, just held

Standing Before You

asking is not losing

God wants to teach me to ask for help
all my life, I have relied on myself

feeling like a burden to others
pieces of a wound
that never heals properly

but, maybe strength is not alone
and healing grows when roots are sown

Standing Before You

what's your verse

i finally understood
what it means
to hold space for emotions
and not to let them devour me
or fall into their loop

but to step back
watching emotions move
like birds flying through

for so long,
i thought sadness meant to stop
that if i felt too much, i'd lose it all

but here's the truth:

your feelings are just visitors
they don't own you

you can feel without drowning
you can observe without spiraling
you can pause without freezing
you can reabsorb and be willing

Standing Before You

people

-it's all about them-

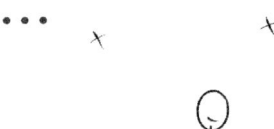

Standing Before You

chapter reflection

sometimes we get so caught up in our thoughts
our worries, our inner world
that we forget there's a bigger world out there
hurting but healing too
the pain might look like ours
some might be different
but it's all real

it's easy to turn inward when things feel heavy
but growth also lives in the looking out
everyone shines in some form
some light in silence
some shine freely
all human

when we lift our face
we see the world isn't just grey
it's layered with colour, memory, desire
there's more out there than just our pain

get curious about the outside
get curious about them

Standing Before You

her

she was 70, and for a while, she looked at me
dreaming of youth and all the things she got to see
she desired to experience it all once again
but deep down, she knew she had no regrets

she had everything she truly desired
a partner who loves her, someone she admires
they were holding hands when i noticed them
sometimes, we long for what we don't possess

let's cherish the moments we have
for life is a gift, a blessing so true
admire others, but appreciate the 'you'
in your own live, let's find grace

thanking God for each day

Standing Before You

we

we are so scared of silence, of pause
we chase after noise just because
we fear what the quiet might bring
we forget that in silence, the heart sings

we need to trust in the calm and the still
we listen to the breeze and let time fill
we find in the hush a thought of you near
we know that silence can hold what we fear

we cherish the quiet where comfort is found
we know that in trust, our souls are unbound
we embrace peace, let go of the hush
we learn that in silence, there's no need to rush

Standing Before You

what they took

someone stole my bag today
they thought it held value
they didn't know what was inside
my work, my wounds, my written life

they took my heart away
alongside pages soaked in pain
years folded into fragile lines
a voice i stitched together again

i stood still, fearful and lost
everything i built, nearly a cost
my dark side, my unmasked face
all almost gone for someone else's take

but by some miracle,
it found its way back to me
untouched, still breathing
like the universe paused to agree

they'll never know
what they almost took…

it was this book

Standing Before You

bond

a dad and daughter trying to reconnect
it's him fighting against his own neglect
in moments shared, they both reflect

they try to make connections
it's sweet to watch
it takes love to make you fulfilled and alive

they try to bridge the silent years
through laughs and talks,
through hopes and fears
each gentle step, a healing touch
each glance exchanged reveals so much

in the end, we're all a bit broken
but love finds ways to make us tokens

Standing Before You

trafficking dreams

you are so direct, but twist the truth
a razor-sharp edge within your youth
hiding scars, you can't explain
trying hard to hide your pain

inside, you rise, are bold, think pure
relentless, forced to endure
your whisper's quiet and slow
no gain from words you can't let go

the law's a game on paper thin
forever stained in hopeless green

there's nowhere left for you to run
your shield is built, and the fight begins

you cut yourself from all you knew
but still, the dreamer keeps shining through

Standing Before You

the curious art of letting go

she once said
'your skin is as soft
as the touch of a cherry blossom
the beauty
it lasts for a season
born to fly away

i want to keep you
forever
but i know at some point
the season will be over

your beauty
is to admire
not to keep
to see you
from a distance
if i touch you
you will fade and
fly away'

you were never mine to hold
but i am grateful i got to see you bloom

and maybe
in another spring
i'll bloom too

stranded youth

the clock never stops
yet she wishes the cake
would last a lifetime

Standing Before You

beauty in difference

scrolling through my feed
i see stories each day
i love seeing you all
in your own special way

different language and skin tones
you inspire me to be more
you make humanity's blend

thank you for being so unique
my dearest and close friends

Standing Before You

our truest form

is it even possible
to be the same person with others
as we are with ourselves?

what we can hold on to
are our values

they're the thread
that keeps us authentic
across every meet cute

we rely on ourselves
because we know how we would
or would not... act
when faced with certain moments

that is our most authentic self:
the one that stays rooted
no matter the room

our personality can shift slightly
reflecting the energy around us
and that's okay

but the core?
it stays

Standing Before You

T.W. apology to the world

in loss, we're brought back to earth
it doesn't feel like a gift, at first anyway
it burns, it humbles, it strips away
that story we told ourselves

sometimes we need the breaking
because without it, we'd never stop
we'd keep running, keep proving
keep feeding the version of us
that the world claps for

failure, as brutal as it feels
is not the opposite of success
it's the door no one wants to open
until life kicks it wide open
and there, in that lonely and quiet place
you finally face yourself

you realise obtaining isn't always growth
and being loved doesn't mean you're whole
you see that even the strongest can lose their way
and sometimes they need to, anyway

because struggle can soften you
it can make you honest
it can make you true

Standing Before You

'believe in you
to keep climbing'
you thought it was the question

but, my dear,
that's the answer

Standing Before You

humanity
is the best poem of all

Standing Before You

her

there's something beautiful
about watching your best friend be loved

love notes stuck to the fridge
love bites on her neck on a
Saturday afternoon
supporting her dreams and obsessions

that kind of love
that kind of truth
leaving a mark in us, too

Standing Before You

the golfer

you hold your breath tight
the ball arcs in morning light
silence spreads across the green
emeralds glitter like a stream

there's a silent prayer in each stroke
holding faith through all you know

infinite walks across the hills
bringing momentary trills
where talks, laughs, and stories untold
are far more precious than the finest gold

Standing Before You

like my grandmother

i want to love like my grandmother
with faith in her bones
and calm in her voice

i want to cook without a recipe
and hum softly while i clean
i want to pray with intention
not out of fear, but gratitude

if i am the flower
she was the root

and because of her i keep blooming

Standing Before You

my neighbour grows sunflowers

i don't know her name, yet
but i know she sings
while she waters her garden
and that her sunflowers bend toward her
like they love her back

that's enough to believe in magic

Standing Before You

mending

she didn't give advice on love
she just sewed the button back on my coat
and asked if i'd eaten

sometimes love isn't loud
it's practical

neglect

Standing Before You

Standing Before You

neglect - chapter reflection

this was the most difficult chapter of the book to write
by now, you've probably noticed
i've been writing reflections after each chapter title...
and this explanation is...

it's me deflecting. stalling
dragging my feet so i don't have to explain it

but ok

it took me some time
to even understand the words:
emotional neglect
let alone say it out loud

emotional neglect
can take many forms
love is complicated and we are human
still, when actions and emotions don't align
the people closest to us can end up hurting us

eventually, as we grow,
it becomes less about what others didn't give us
and more about us asking:

what am i missing? and why?
we want to be seen and held

this part is about learning
(and sometimes failing)
to give ourselves the love we wanted
or how we wanted it
to prevent us from running on empty

Standing Before You

care given

hidden wounds masked by unstable disguise
hiding your pain yet reaching the skies
what i need from you, i know i can't get
a shoulder to cry on, not hidden regret

shame is a gift when i open my heart
sharing my tears, tears me apart
you see in me what you bury inside
reflecting scars in places we hide

the person i love, the source of my pain
a cycle of hurt, two storms in the rain

yet, here i remain
thought broken and torn
i'm hoping in time
self-love will reborn

Standing Before You

if no one shows love
we will walk through life
emotionally neglected
wanting to feel connected

let's break the cycle
and start acknowledging the true…

… what we all want is to love and be loved too

Standing Before You

the mirror and the mask

when we look in the mirror
and what we see are flaws
a reflection blurred by a silent pause
not the same as when you look at them
where love and light shine through

so much compassion for the rest
but for ourselves, there's no kindness left
making excuses when you see their pain
yet leave your own to fall like rain

the mirror shows what you can't defend
a heart so willing to bend for a friend

but in this glass, you stand alone
a stranger to love, but you were never shown

Standing Before You

self

no compassion for self
but plenty for others
trying to fix you while losing my power

letting your flaws go, holding a spear for me
fighting my battles, yet letting you be free

i am happy i am drawing a line
setting boundaries, reclaiming what's mine
putting myself first, opening my eyes
this time i'll rise, coming first this time

Standing Before You

to my next

the feeling of being safe
the feeling of being understood
the feeling of being supported
it makes me stand for what's true

even on bad days, we stay connected
in love. in lust. we feel respected
with this letter, i send to the sun
at peace, my journey began

i've worked so deep to find my way
i feel worthy; i'm proud today

Standing Before You

in the past

someone asked me what i seek in a partner
once it was the broken, to play the saviour
losing myself in the love i would display
now, i know i deserve a brighter way

Standing Before You

my mother, silently loved

she never said "i'm proud"
but she saved the space intact after I left the house
she asked if i was ok
to be cautious when falling in love
she thought of me
even when we didn't speak for a while

i see now
her kind of love was a language
i had to learn slowly

allow yourself to feel the hurt
love yourself and let 'her' go

Standing Before You

stop

i don't even want to write anymore
i'm changing so much
with each chapter i explore

it's scary to be a chameleon
and not being able to change the interior

i must confess
i've enjoyed pouring the pain
but there's no need to be broken
to let the words reign

Standing Before You

i may still refuse

you must trust someone
i know it's hard
but you'll find it's worthwhile
even when you're sad
though they may fail you
don't let it dismay you

…trust can bring light to the darkest of days

loneliness

what's loneliness, i ask me?

how does it feel?
how deep is the ache?

it's going from town to town
thinking no one truly cares
it's being surrounded by people
yet wishing to be elsewhere

it's the weight that keeps you in bed
the past, present, and future…
…all missing, never there

it's the wounds you refuse to seal
the excuses are never real

it's holding on to heartbreak
it's refusing to experience life
it's longing for peace of mind

Standing Before You

i want someone who is whole
as i loved what is broken

i want someone that's kind
as i loved heartbroken

i want someone who supports me
as I loved those who don't see me

i want someone who's open
as i loved softspoken

i want to find true love
as i loved the tears
redefining the meaning
and putting behind my fears

i will be kind, whole and ready
for when you want to come along and be steady

i will be patient in my waiting
for i have learned to stand alone
when the time is right
our love will be carved in stone

Standing Before You

hard...

...rescue

when the energy is at its lowest
you tried so hard to be flawless
when you get home, and the room is empty
you don't know what part, but you feel dented

these are parts of you that were neglected
when you were young and needed to be protected

the love you needed coming to the surface
all those years you silently suffered

asking yourself for a hug can save you
it might sound sad, but say: 'i missed you'

Standing Before You

gift yourself the softness
you never received

Standing Before You

letter*s*

-to God, to myself, to strangers, to the universe-

Standing Before You

Standing Before You

God... make me a better daughter
true
with a kinder heart, reflecting You

help me find my place
feel the peace in the air
in those moments when my faith fades

help me grow and reflect Your love
gentle
as all the stars above

help me stop the judgment
that blinds my sight
let me see love in Your light

not to mold others to my will
but to grow my love and feel fulfilled

with patience and peace, a calm mind...
guide my steps. Your path to find

Standing Before You

breathe, love
you've come so far
not perfect, just human
with a wild, soft heart

rest when you need
rise when you want
and never forget
you're doing the best you can

Standing Before You

to the person that invented coffee

THANK YOU

Standing Before You

my face reveals what i won't say
expressions speak in a crowded way
but deep inside, i keep it all
a quiet heart behind a wall

disposable love

one of my biggest fears
is being the disposable one
the one you meet one night
and forget the next
not built for it, yet i've been there
not built for it, but i admire my strength

Standing Before You

i love your strength
and how you handle conflict

Standing Before You

in an empty room
our eyes connected
a fleeting spark
can't be mistaken
no words exchanged
no names to know
yet for a moment
i fiercely glowed

the hum of the world faded away
your silence begged me to stay
a glance of fate
a whispered of chance
lost in the current
of a promised land

but

you slipped away
the moment passed
no numbers asked
no promises said

i long for love and now, after you, i want more

for thought you are gone
the spark remains
the mystery will stay mixed in my vains

Standing Before You

if you are around death, create life

it will save you...

Standing Before You

what's the feeling i should have
when i see my reflection?

Standing Before You

some days won't go well
you will miss the world outside
it will be you with clouds in your mind

the windows won't open
including the ones of your soul
you will want to stay hidden
never walk past those doors

your own voice will be the enemy
and you know this happens often

look for comfort
in those who speak to you with love and kindness

don't listen to yourself, listen to your friends

it's crazy to think they know you better
than you know yourself

Standing Before You

when you sit in my lap
its like God is hugging me
lightening some of the pain
making me feel less lonely

to fox

Standing Before You

understanding ourselves takes a while
we go through so much pain
building who we are out of fire

we burn but ashes can rebuild
our soul can be stronger
that we might think

Standing Before You

i know how tired you are
of holding it all together
of being brave when no one is watching
of carrying the weight of justice, of culture, of womanhood
all while still trying to write something soft

i have been told to shrink
to stay quiet, to prove myself
i have stood in rooms where my name
accent, my truth
were too much or not enough

but i stayed anyway. i stood

i am not the roles i had to play
i am not the job they took away
or the silence they offered in return

i am the fire, the faith, the poetry, the verse

healing isn't loud, and neither am i
i do it quietly, page by page
with sticky notes on my wall
and a green heart for every soul i touch

i've given love that wasn't returned
i've stayed kind when they were cruel
i've wrote books out of pain
and hope out of heartbreak

i forgive me for the times i stayed too long
i honour me for the days i walked away
i see the girl who didn't get washed away
and the woman who's learning
to give it to herself anyway

Standing Before You

i am allowed to rest
i am allowed to cry
and even if no one ever says it
the way i want

i love you. i'm staying

keep going

-me-

Standing Before You

i like the colour green
when it means growth
i like words that bleed honestly
and faces that don't hide feelings at all
i like post it leaves on my wall
one for every soul who reads my heart

i like days that feel cinematic
i like eyes that sparkle with understanding
and people who don't need a script to be kind

i like sexy names
and star signs that explain a lot
I like when people pause
i like being all-or-nothing, even when it hurts

i like the idea of love showing up for me
i like the silence that comes after a long day
i like the chaos that leads to art
i like looking good, feeling good, being loyal

i like film sets and stories that never end
i like reels that mean something
and dms i shouldn't have sent

i like being Venezuelan
i like when someone gets me
i like being seen. fully. not half empty

i like writing books that remember pain
and when they end in survival
i like being soft and powerful
emotional and intentional
sexy, sometimes, and soulful all the time

Standing Before You

waking up

i think I am, now, waking up
from a long dream called youth
there are so many things
i wish i had done differently…
but it's like i wasn't here

not fully

just moving through life
feeling, reacting, hoping
but not seeing
like i was sleepwalking through years
that mattered more than i realised

and now, the strange work of being an adult
is trying to remember that child i once was
to go back, somehow
to what was real before i forgot

Standing Before You

wishful thinking

no stars tonight
just that spark in your eyes
looking at me with no rest
i am wondering if i should tell
the secret i hold so true
that i love everything you do

Standing Before You

like you

i am searching for a man like you
where your thoughts run deep
and sometimes blue
your dark eyes, with stories untold
a weathered heart, both bruised and bold
willing to try just one more time
carrying lessons like subtle lines

i see your past, i see it clearly
and all i want is to draw you near
but chances passed us, like Christmas might
moments were missed in the quiet night

unspoken words, untaken hands
opportunities lost in shifting wands

that smile still lights the darkened skies
i wonder, if you realised

in all the quiet, all the mist
do you ever think about the what ifs?
of what could have been, what slipped away
the things we never got to say

Standing Before You

our way of loving
is not absolute

Standing Before You

when no one claps

healing is lonely work
especially when no one sees it

but every time you choose peace over panic
presence over performance
or softness over shame
you are winning

without applause but full of power

español

Este libro fue escrito en inglés,
pero algunas páginas tuvieron que nacer en español
porque donde sea que voy, me llevo lo que soy:

-VENEZOLANA-

. . .

Standing Before You

Standing Before You

si pudiera recordar con más nitidez
cómo sonaba mi risa al jugar en la niñez
cómo eran mis pasos, torpes y sinceros
cómo brillaban mis ojos al ver los luceros

si pudiera mirar sin niebla el pasado
ver a mi madre con sueños aún no contados
sentarme a su lado, ser su confidente
decirle: "no estás sola, aquí estoy, presente"

si pudiera bailar con mi abuela soltera
preguntarle en secreto qué amores tuviera
si alguna vez dudó, si alguna vez lloró
y si también soñaba con quien no llegó

si pudiera abrazar a mi padre de niño
y ver en su risa mi propio cariño
jugar con su sombra, correr a su lado
ver al hombre fuerte
siendo apenas un chiquillo encantado

qué distinto sería este mapa del alma
si tuviéramos más memorias con calma
si no se borraran los días dorados
bajo el peso sutil de los años pasados

pero quizás, en lo que no se recuerda
vive el misterio que el corazón observa
y en cada gesto mío, en mi forma de amar
vive un eco de ellos, sin necesidad de buscar

así, aunque no vi todo lo que anhelo
llevo su historia tatuada en el cielo
y con cada paso que doy, sin saber
ellos caminan conmigo, sin desaparecer

padre

la cobija que calienta
la protección que revienta
todo sentido de desilusión

ayudas a mi corazón
a entender y sentir amor

como la estrella que guía el camino
como el lucero que crea mi destino

es la pausa que das
para escuchar mis problemas
dejando atrás todos tus dilemas

respiro y ya estás orgulloso
gracias por ser tan luminoso

Standing Before You

positivo

gracias a Dios por la familia que me has dado
por ellos veo bondad en todos lados

estudio valores, exploro verdades
y en ellos confío, sin vanidades

cómo ven la vida, cómo cuidan los animales
cómo tratan a su gente, con actos tan leales

gracias a Dios por mi familia querida
mi refugio seguro en un mundo de heridas

luchadores incansables, corazones presentes
con pensamientos brillantes, nunca ausentes

con ternura latente y un corazón guerrero
dispuestos a salvar el mundo entero

gracias por enseñarme a evaluar acciones
y a actuar siempre con buenas intenciones

a ser buena gente, con tres dedos de frente
a tener un alma ardiente y sueños en mente

creer en el rezo, en estar contenta
en el poder del amor, siempre atenta

dar cobijo al necesitado
perdonar y dejar el pasado

momentos

la felicidad es un segundo
un destello fugaz de luz
la pieza perfecta de mármol
perdida en la mirada del escultor

al final, desaparece
se funde con lo que fue
un diente de león en la brisa
un recuerdo que pasó
la felicidad se desvanece cuando se agarra

como el paso del tiempo,
como la arena que se desplaza
una búsqueda, no un destino
un viaje, no un lugar
nada cambia realmente

guarda la persecución interminable
abraza la alegría o la tristeza
en cada respiración que tomas
este momento fugaz
lo atesoraré contigo

un segundo de pura felicidad
un destello de algo verdadero

Standing Before You

moverse

si se necesita movimiento
para crear acción
¿por qué tenemos tanto miedo
de avanzar, creando tracción?

la acción exige que dejemos de lado la duda
lejos del silencio, y demos un paso audaz
¿es lo desconocido lo que nos mantiene en su lugar
las sombras del fracaso ¿tememos enfrentarlas?

en la quietud admiramos el camino por delante
sueños aún por vivir, tantas palabras sin decir
tal vez es la comodidad de lo que ahora conocemos
lo familiar, la rutina en la que crecemos despacio
entonces, ¿por qué temblamos ante la idea de lo nuevo?
olvidamos que el coraje puede llevarnos alto

al final:

es el movimiento lo que da forma a nuestro destino
el miedo es solo algo que debemos mitigar

levantémonos entonces con amor en el corazón
abracemos lo desconocido a medida que cada viaje
comienza

porque la acción es vida
y la vida es moverse

Standing Before You

tienes a ti mismo

en la ausencia de apoyo externo
el amor que tienes por ti mismo
usualmente viene en su forma más pura
ya que nadie más estuvo allí para ti
excepto tú mismo

lo lograrás

Standing Before You

si eres afortunado
y trabajas lo suficiente
te convertirás en el guardián
que una vez anhelaste…
…y eso es hermoso

música y ejercicio

la música y el ejercicio
son mis constantes salvadoras
en este breve viaje
donde las mentes chocan

me han salvado mil veces
levantado mi alma
mantuvieron mi corazón latiendo
me mantuvieron, más o menos, entero

cuando las sombras persisten
y la esperanza parece delgada
una canción o una carrera me devuelve

el ritmo hace latir mi corazón
liberándome... despertándome
desbloqueando la fuerza profunda en mis huesos

en melodías duermo
y en movimientos, desperté
encuentro la paz que necesito para crecer

a través de altos y bajos
iluminan el camino
salvándome aún, día tras día

desafío

desafía quién eres
desafía tus opiniones
conviértete en una fuerza única
sé uno en un millón

absorbe los puntos de vista
que vienen de todas direcciones
identifica tus defectos
estamos exentos de la perfección

Standing Before You

trabajar en ti mismo...
¿qué significa realmente?

es encontrar las piezas rotas que tienes por dentro,
invisibles.
leer, aprender, romperte un poco más...
...para que todas las piezas rotas se vuelvan a ordenar.

al final, sabrás lo que quieres
quién eres y tendrás un plan

estar 'roto' es solo el comienzo de un nuevo destino

no te rindas

Standing Before You

dar cobijo al necesitado
perdonar y dejar el pasado

arrecho

no sé cómo hacemos
para estar lejos de nuestra familia por tanto tiempo
y seguir adelante con una sonrisa

¿será que estamos en piloto automático
o es nuestra esencia de luchadores?

siento un amor tan profundo por la vida
por el bienestar de todos, por lograr mis sueños
y seguir adelante

pero el pensar que el huequito en el corazón
más bien se expande, pero gracias a ellos
tenemos el corazón bien grande

Standing Before You

respira mi cielo

has llegado tan lejos
no perfecta, solo humana
con un corazón salvaje y tierno

descansa cuando lo necesites
levántate cuando quieras
y nunca olvides:

estás haciendo lo mejor que puedes

Standing Before You

como mis abuelas

quiero amar como mi abuela
con fe en los huesos
y calma en la voz
quiero cocinar sin mirar la receta
y cantar bajito mientras limpio
quiero rezar con intención
no por miedo, sino por gratitud

si soy la flor
ella fue la raíz
y por ellas… sigo floreciendo

Standing Before You

estoy aprendiendo a quedarme

estoy aprendiendo a quedarme
cuando mi corazón quiere huir
a sentarme con el silencio
en vez de convertirme en él

por mucho tiempo
convertí la ausencia en amor
pensé que si desaparecía
quizá alguien me buscaría
pero ahora me doy presencia a mí misma
digo mi nombre con ternura
abrazo el dolor hasta que se ablande

esta vez, no mendigo migajas
no me encojo para encajar
nutro las partes de mí
que otros olvidaron alimentar

ya no estoy vacía
sólo estoy en construcción
pero estoy aprendiendo a quedarme
y amarme con devoción

Standing Before You

el espejo y la máscara

he usado mil versiones de mí
solo para no mostrar quién soy

la feliz
la fuerte
la que no siente
la que no pide

pero el espejo no miente
y mis ojos ya no quieren mentir tampoco

no quiero esconderme detrás de la sonrisa
ni justificar por qué siento tanto
ya no

si tengo que ser amada
que sea por lo que realmente soy
con todo y todo

Standing Before You

por fin entendí
lo que significa sostener espacio para mis emociones
no dejar que me devoren
no caer en su ruido
sino dar un paso atrás
observarlas pasar

como clima en un cielo que aún me pertenece
antes pensaba que la tristeza era derrota

pero ahora sé:

es solo una visitante
no mi dueña
no mi nombre

puedo sentir sin ahogarme
observar sin caer en espiral
pausar sin congelarme

la acción me salva
cada vez
un respiro
un paso
una palabra que temía decir
pero necesitaba
sostener el espacio

no es silencio
es suavidad
y fuerza
al mismo tiempo

Standing Before You

querida yo,

sé lo cansada que estás de sostenerlo todo
de ser fuerte, dulce, lista, y callada al mismo tiempo
has vivido mil vidas solo por querer ser entendida

pero ahora te veo
de verdad

esto no es el final
es el entretiempo
la parte del camino donde sanar se siente incierto
y tener coraje significa quedarte, aunque duela

no estás atrasada
no estás rota
estás construyendo

te perdono por las veces que no soñaste más
me enorgullezco de ti por las veces que sí dormiste

y aunque nadie lo diga como tú lo necesitas
yo te amo
yo me quedo

sigue adelante

Standing Before You

razones para quedarte

el sol no te pidió que sonrías hoy
solo salió
suave, dorado, callado
como tú

tu respiración ya es prueba
de que hay algo por lo que vale la pena quedarse
aunque no sepas qué es todavía

quédate por el café, la música, el viento
por el libro sin terminar
por ti

Standing Before You

repite esto cuando olvides quién eres

no tengo que correr para valer
no tiene que doler para existir
no tengo que demostrar mi valor
a quien no puede verlo

no tengo que encajar donde no hay espacio para mí
no soy demasiado
ni demasiado intensa
ni muy suave
ni muy fuerte

soy lo que soy
y eso es sagrado

Standing Before You

regálate la suavidad que nunca recibiste

regálate la suavidad
que te negaron cuando más la necesitabas

háblate con ternura
aunque no estés bien
abraza tus días sin energía
sin juzgarte por no brillar

haz pausas sin culpa
cuida tu cuerpo como si fuese un jardín
aunque nadie te enseñó cómo
aunque a veces olvides que lo mereces

regálate lo que pediste en silencio
y verás que empiezas a sanar

Standing Before You

el golfista

siempre contienes el aliento
viendo tu tiro dibujar un arco en la mañana
el silencio se extiende por el césped
que parecen esmeraldas que brillan en un arroyo

hay una oración silenciosa en cada golpe
sosteniendo fe en todo
caminatas infinitas por las colinas
trayendo momentos de añoro
donde charlas, risas y lo no dicho,
son mucho más preciosos que el oro

Standing Before You

cuando nadie aplaude

sanar es un trabajo solitario
especialmente cuando nadie lo ve

pero cada vez que eliges paz en vez de pánico
presencia en vez de actuar
o ternura en vez de vergüenza
estás ganando

sin aplausos, pero con poder

Standing Before You

mi vecina cultiva girasoles

no sé su nombre
pero canta mientras riega su jardín
y los girasoles se inclinan hacia ella
como si la amaran también

eso me basta para creer otra vez
en las cosas suaves

Standing Before You

el secreto de la vida

creo que el error que cometemos
es pensar que debemos elegir
entre el caos y la paz
entre la vejez y la juventud

siento que el secreto de la vida
es hacer las paces con ambos
en la dualidad está la vida
y estamos llenos de los dos

un equilibrio a la vista
es lo que debemos abrazar
el toque pacífico de plumas en el rostro
cuando el fuego quema los talones

Standing Before You

puedes sentir sin ahogarte

tus sentimientos son solo visitantes
no son tus dueños
no son tu nombre

puedes sentir sin ahogarte

Standing Before You

por cierto, que bonita es la letra ñ

Standing Before You

finalmente

solía esconderme detrás de la fuerza
palabras filosas
respuestas perfectas
una sonrisa que sabía el guion

pero algo cambió
cuando dejé que las grietas
hablaran por mí

cuando permití que el silencio
dijera más de lo que la defensa jamás podría

cuando dije
así soy yo
y dejé que el eco
cayera donde quisiera

Standing Before You

final note to you

you made it to the end
and i can't be more grateful

that means something

maybe you recognised pieces of yourself
in one of these pages

i hope this book reminded you
that even when things feel difficult
we all know life can be hard, but still
you still have the power to stand

and maybe, just maybe
you already are

thank you for letting me be here…

standing before you

nota
llegaste al final
y no puedo estar más agradecida.
quizá reconociste partes de ti
en alguna de estas páginas.
espero que este libro te haya recordado
que incluso cuando todo se siente difícil,
y todas sabemos que la vida puede ser dura,
aún tienes el poder de levantarte.

gracias por dejarme estar aquí…
de pie ante ti

Standing Before You

Book one of the 'before you' series

Crumbling Before You

digging deep sounds scary
more when all your life,
your feelings have been buried.
so many people took advantage of you
but deep down, you already knew
why did you ignore all the signs? i wonder...
choosing the direct path to rain and thunder
ego, pride? all the wrong reasons
finding love that only lasts a season

page 71

available on www.amazon.com
scan the qr code

Standing Before You

thank you

to those who stood beside me in my silence
who held space when i didn't have the words
thank you

to my family, chosen or given
for teaching me what love looks like
even in its imperfectly perfect form

to my friends, who believed in me
before i believed in myself
thank you

to every stranger who smiled,
every message that came at the right time,
and every kind soul who saw me

to my beautiful Venezuela and Scotland.
both *home*
thank you

to you, the reader who picked this book
and saw something familiar. i see you too

to whoever discovered coffee & to my cat. thank you

lastly, to the version of me who kept writing
even in the dark, you are never alone

a Dios. GRACIAS!

with all my heart
Maholi xoxo

Standing Before You

Daily Journal

this journal will walk with you
a space to capture your quiet thoughts
write the unspoken truth
to find strength in your vulnerability

this is your story, unfolding

scan the qr code

available on www.amazon.com

if this book moved you, consider leaving a review on amazon. it helps others find these words when they need them most

Standing Before You

Book Recommendation
Spanish

Oswaldo Díaz nacido en tierras venezolanas nos lleva al mundo de la prosa convertida en expresión de sentimientos y situaciones humanas que nos conducen a la meditación y reflexión sobre la vida.

Prosas y Otras Cosas de Oswaldo Díaz

www.amazon.com

&

Running on Empty. Book by Dr. Jonice Webb

Standing Before You

About the Author

Maholi Díaz is a Venezuelan-born writer and creative who has called Scotland home since 2017.

she writes blending emotional honesty with lyrical prose to explore identity, healing, love, and resilience.

her work speaks to those navigating quiet battles offering comfort, clarity, and the reminder that softness is strength.

Standing Before You is her second book, following *Crumbling Before You*, and is part of a larger journey of transformation and self-trust.

when she's not writing, Maholi finds joy in music, sipping strong coffee while imagining better futures.

Instagram: **@maholi.diaz**

Printed in Dunstable, United Kingdom